Englisch-Stars
3

Comics

Erarbeitet von

Barbara Gleich
Irene Reindl
Katrin Schmidt
Britta Schöpe

Illustriert von

Wilfried Poll

Cornelsen

Inhalt

New colours for Sally . . . 3

Who likes lollipops? 6

An art lesson 9

A walk at night 12

Money for new toys 15

Sally's patchwork
dress 18

Rainy holidays 21

Pool party 24

A game with drinks 27

Sally's special
breakfast 30

Eating a rainbow 33

All my pets 36

Fun outside 39

I want to ride a... 42

Hide-and-seek in
London 45

Quiz 48

📕 Comic

New colours for Sally

✏️ 1. Draw lines.

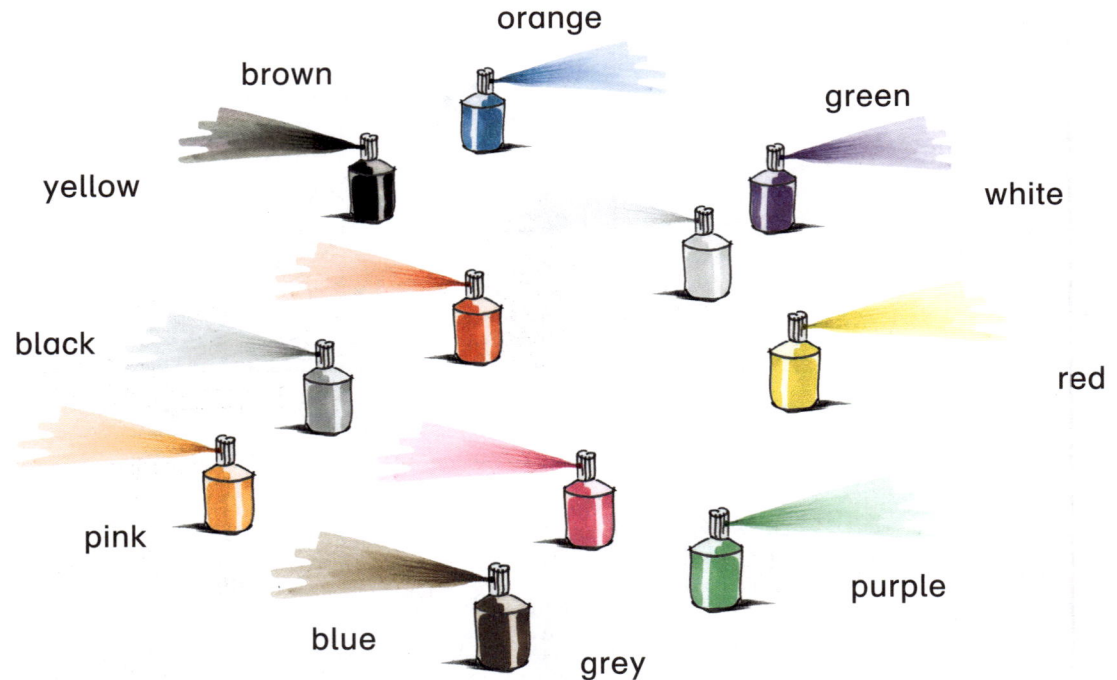

orange

brown

green

yellow

white

black

red

pink

purple

blue

grey

✏️ 2. Write.

I'm _____

and _____.

I'm _____

and _____.

I'm _____

and _____.

I'm _____

and _____.

In welchen Farben sind die Gesichter der Kinder geschminkt?

4

3. Correct or wrong? Look, read and tick.

4. How do you like Sally best? Colour and write.

That's great. I'm _____.

📖 Comic

Who likes lollipops?

We have got **one** loaf of bread, **two** bottles of milk and **three** oranges.

Four bananas.

Five apples.

What's that, Billy? **Six** lollipops? No, Billy!

Seven, eight rolls.

And a package with **nine** chocolate bars.

Oh no, Billy, not again. **Ten** lollipops?

Please, Mum.

Wow! Thank you, Billy. I love lollipops.

1. Circle the words and write.

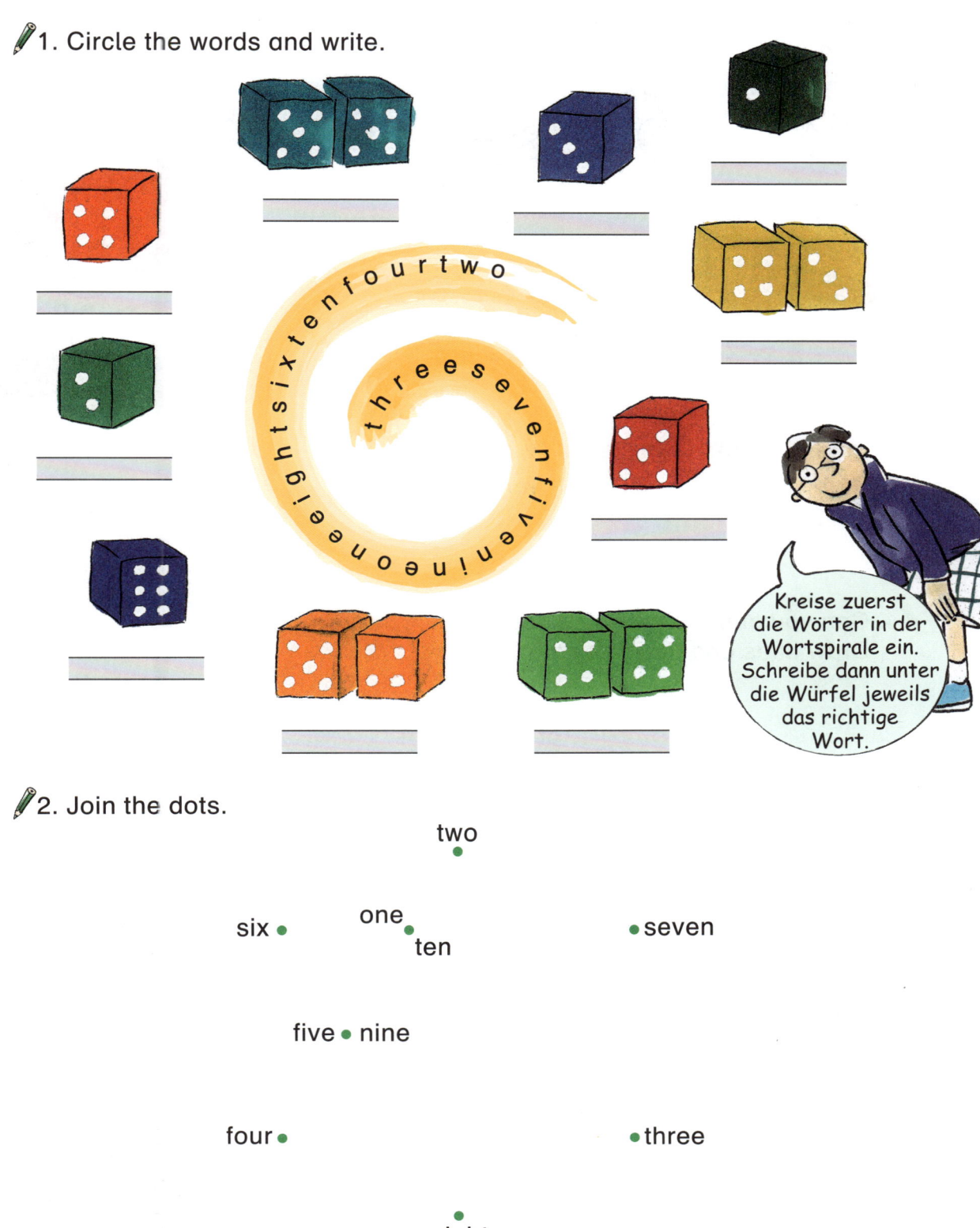

Kreise zuerst die Wörter in der Wortspirale ein. Schreibe dann unter die Würfel jeweils das richtige Wort.

2. Join the dots.

two

six   one   seven
        ten

five • nine

four •   • three

eight

3. How many of these things do Billy and his mum buy? Write.

_____ _____ _____ _____

> Wie viel der jeweils abgebildeten Sachen kaufen Billy und seine Mutter?

_____ _____ _____ Billy buys _____ .

one	**two**	**three**	**four**
five	**eight**	**nine**	**ten**

4. Can you answer the questions?
   Draw lines and find the word.

> One purple, two purple, three purple lollipops,
>
> four purple, five purple, six purple lollipops,
>
> seven purple, eight purple, nine purple lollipops,
>
> ten lollipops for me!

Billy and his mum are	at school. (n) at home. (z) at the supermarket. (f)
They buy	three oranges. (o) six oranges. (i) nine oranges. (e)
Billy buys	ten lollipops. (u) five lollipops. (n) eight lollipops. (r)
The lollipops are for	Mum. (e) Billy. (o) Sally. (r)

The word is: _____

Comic

An art lesson

1. Look and write.

	1	2	3
A			
B			
C			
D			

Suche das Feld in der Tabelle und schreibe das richtige Wort in die Zeile

B2 _____

A1 _____

D3 _____

B3 _____

C2 _____

D1 _____

C3 _____

C1 _____

A3 _____

B1 _____

D2 _____

A2 _____

scissors   rubber   schoolbag   pencil case

water colours   picture   folder

glue   book   pen   ruler   pencil

2. Find the word and draw.

enp	lurer	berbru
eulg	srosciss	cinpel

Entziffere das Wort und male den Gegenstand.

3. What dc Sally and Koala need for their art lesson? Tick the correct answers.

◯ pen ◯ coloured pencils ◯ book ◯ rubber ◯ ruler

◯ folder ◯ water colours ◯ pencil case ◯ scissors ◯ glue

4. Number the pictures in the correct order. Draw lires.

I don't like it.

Nummeriere die Bilder in der richtigen Reihenfolge. Verbinde dann mit der passenden Sprechblase.

That's a great picture of my best friend.

Can I have your grey pencil, please?

📕 Comic

A walk at night

✏ 1. Write and draw.

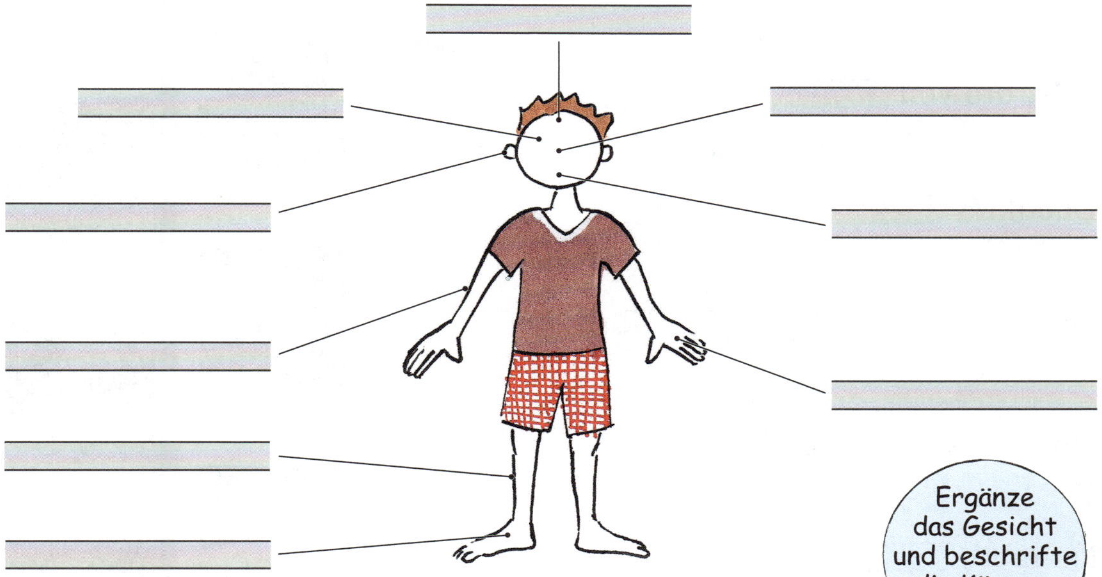

Ergänze
das Gesicht
und beschrifte
die Körper-
teile.

head	eyes	mouth	ears	nose
legs	arms	hands	foot/feet	

✏ 2. How do they feel? Do the crossword.

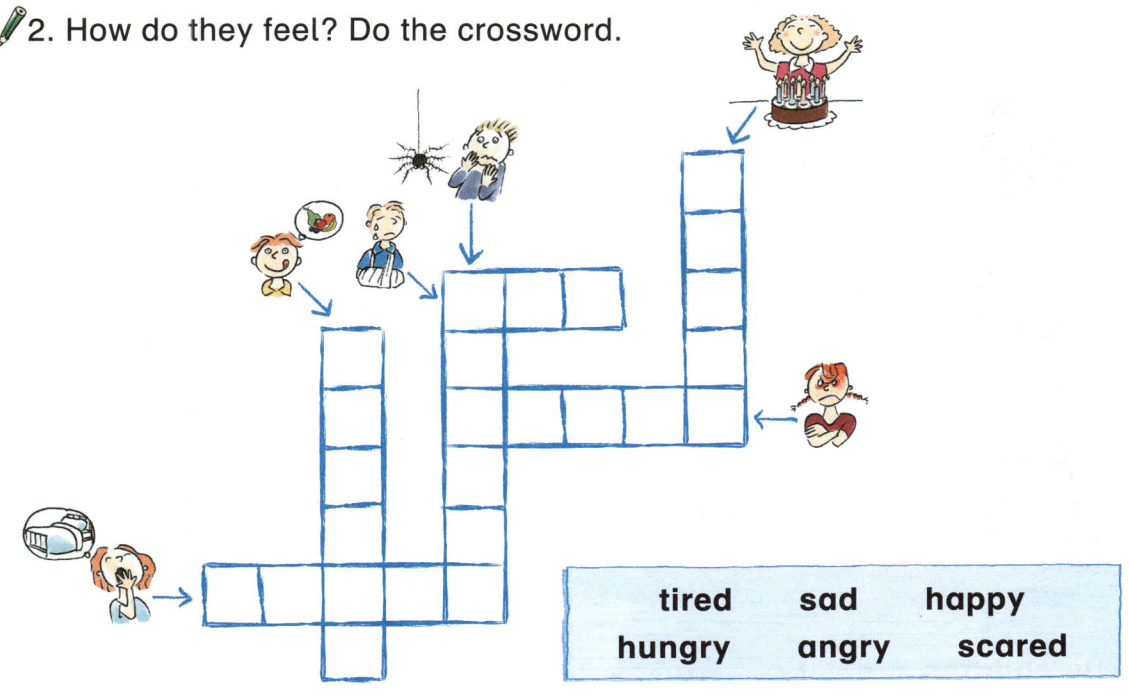

tired	sad	happy
hungry	angry	scared

3. Look at the comic and complete the sentences. Draw lines.

Lilly, are you _____?

Ouch! My _____!

I can see _____.

Oh, look at the long _____!

I'm really _____ now.

I'm so _____ it was only a rabbit.

4. Draw lines and circle the correct letter.
   Find out, how the children feel.

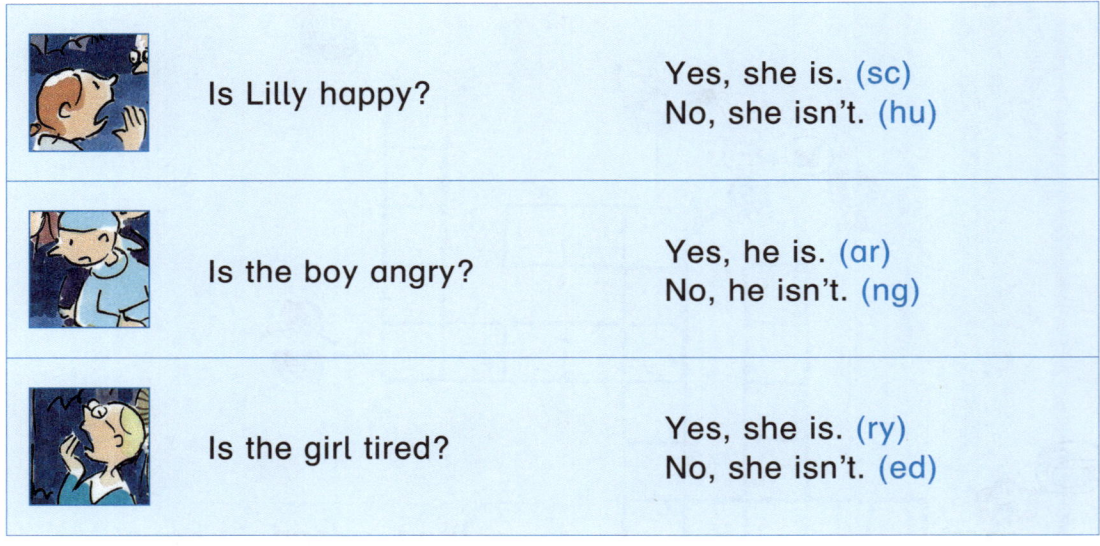

	Is Lilly happy?	Yes, she is. (sc) No, she isn't. (hu)
	Is the boy angry?	Yes, he is. (ar) No, he isn't. (ng)
	Is the girl tired?	Yes, she is. (ry) No, she isn't. (ed)

The children are very _____.

📕 Comic

Money for new toys

1. Where are the toys? Look and write.

	1	2	3
A	doll	castle	spaceship
B	lorry	racing car	ball
C	inline skates	teddy bear	train

Schreibe zuerst auf, in welchem Feld sich jeweils der Gegenstand befindet. Trage unten dann die Wörter richtig ein.

In which square...

is the **lorry**? __B1__

is the **castle**? _____

is the **spaceship**? _____

is the **train**? _____

is the **ball**? _____

is the **doll**? _____

is the **racing car**? _____

are the **inline skates**? _____

is the **teddy bear**? _____

_____

_____

_____

_____

_____

_____

_____

_____

_____

2. Match the sentences with the correct person. Draw lines.

We don't need a new doll and
a new racing car.

Let's do a flea market
and sell some toys.

How much are the castle and
the teddy bear?

You have so many toys.
I'm not buying anything else for you.

How much are the ball and the train?

We need money for the doll and
the racing car.

3. What's wrong in the pictures? Write.

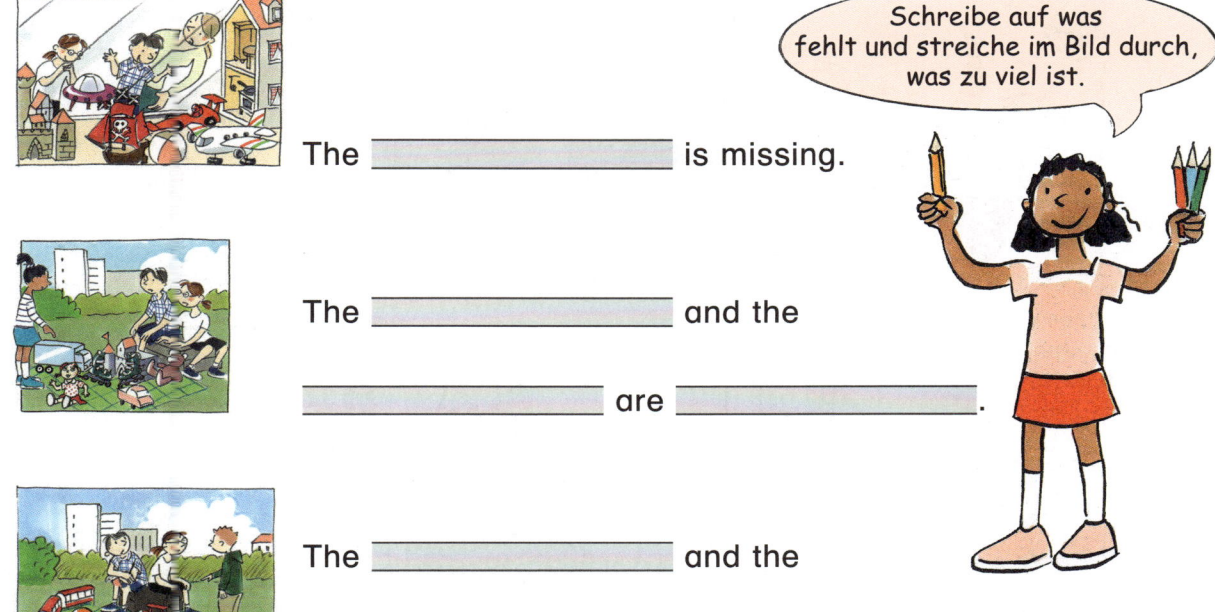

The _____ is missing.

The _____ and the

_____ are _____ .

The _____ and the

_____ are _____ .

Schreibe auf was
fehlt und streiche im Bild durch,
was zu viel ist.

17

 Comic

Sally's patchwork dress

Great! Tina wants me to come to her birthday party.

Birthday party ♡

I don't know what to wear to the party.

The yellow dress is too small, the red skirt is too big and the blue blouse is too old.

I've got an idea!

That looks nice. I like my new dress.

Mummy, can you help me, please?

I'm off to Tina's party now. Thank you, Mummy, you are great.

18

1. What can you see? Write.

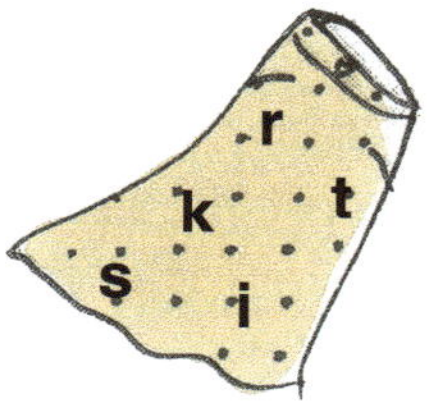

_____

_____

_____

_____

_____

_____

_____

_____

| T-shirt | anorak | skirt | pullover | trousers |
| blouse | dress | shoes |

2. Do the clothes fit? Draw lines and write.

The **pullover** is **too small** .

The **skirt** is **just right** .

The **shoes** are **too big** .

The **blouse** is **too old** .

3. Tick the correct answer.

Sally wants to go	to school. shopping. to Tina's birthday party.	○ ○ ○
Sally wants	a dress. a coat. a pair of trousers.	○ ○ ○
The red skirt is	too small. too old. too big.	○ ○ ○
Sally	likes her new dress. doesn't like her new dress. likes her old dress.	○ ○ ○

4. Number the sentences in the correct order.

○ I don't know what to wear to the party.

○ I'm off to Tina's party now. Thank you, Mummy, you are great.

○ Mummy, can you help me, please?

○ I've got an idea!

○ The yellow dress is too small, the red skirt is too big and the blue blouse is too old.

○ Great! Tina wants me to come to her birthday party.

○ That looks nice. I like my new dress.

20

📕 Comic

Rainy holidays

1. What's the weather like? Write.

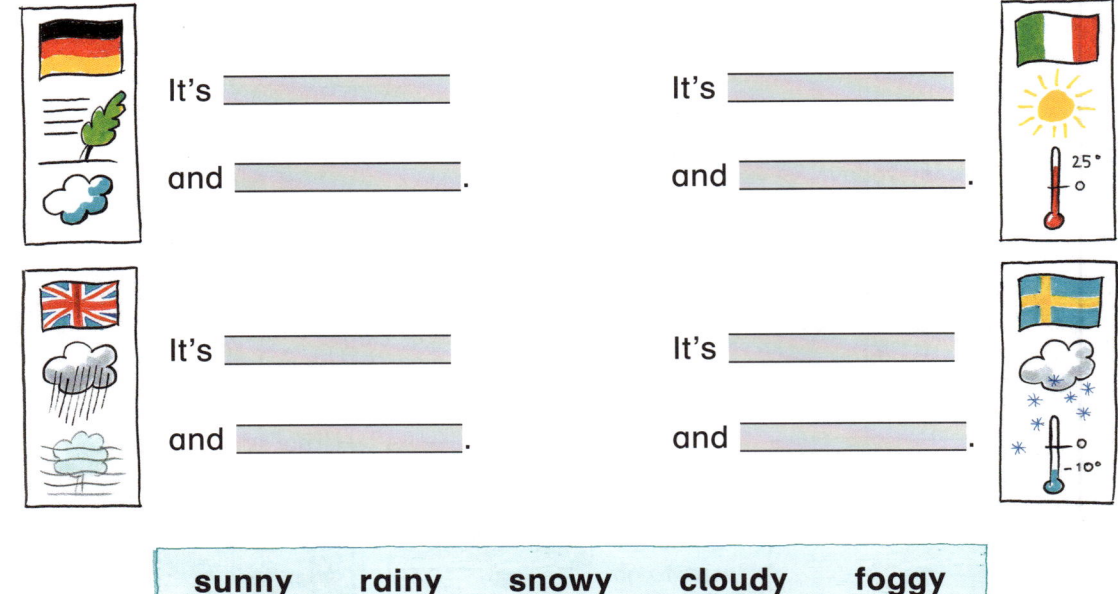

sunny	rainy	snowy	cloudy	foggy
	windy	cold	hot	

2. Find the words and number in the correct order.

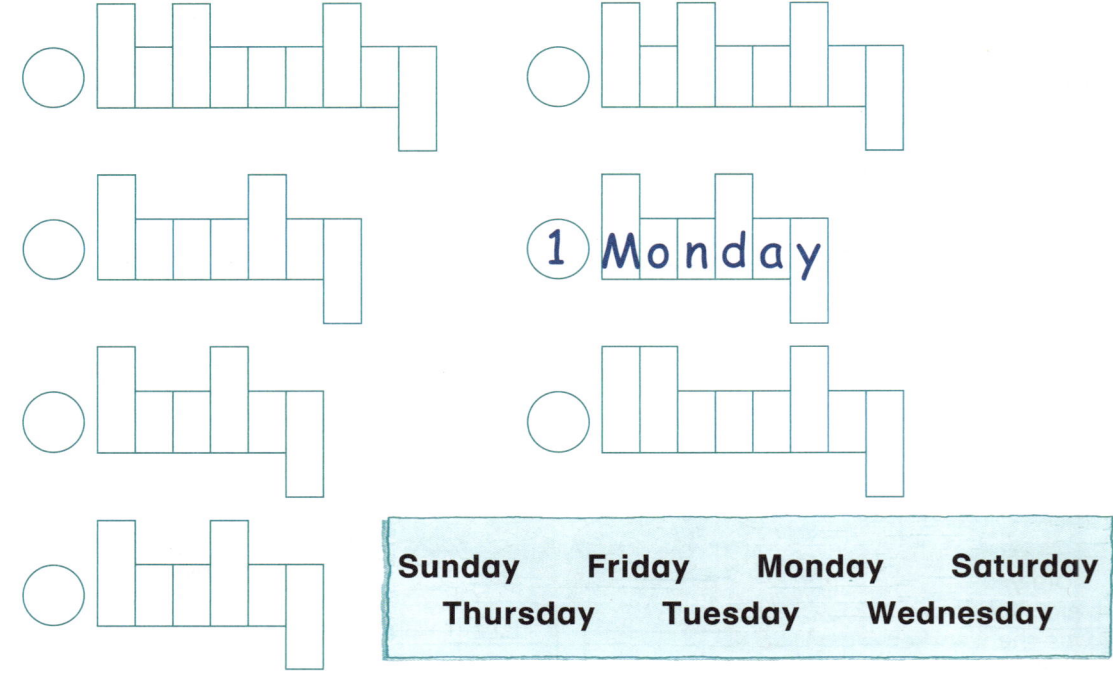

① Monday

Sunday	Friday	Monday	Saturday
Thursday	Tuesday	Wednesday	

1₂3 3. Number the pictures in the correct order. Find the word.

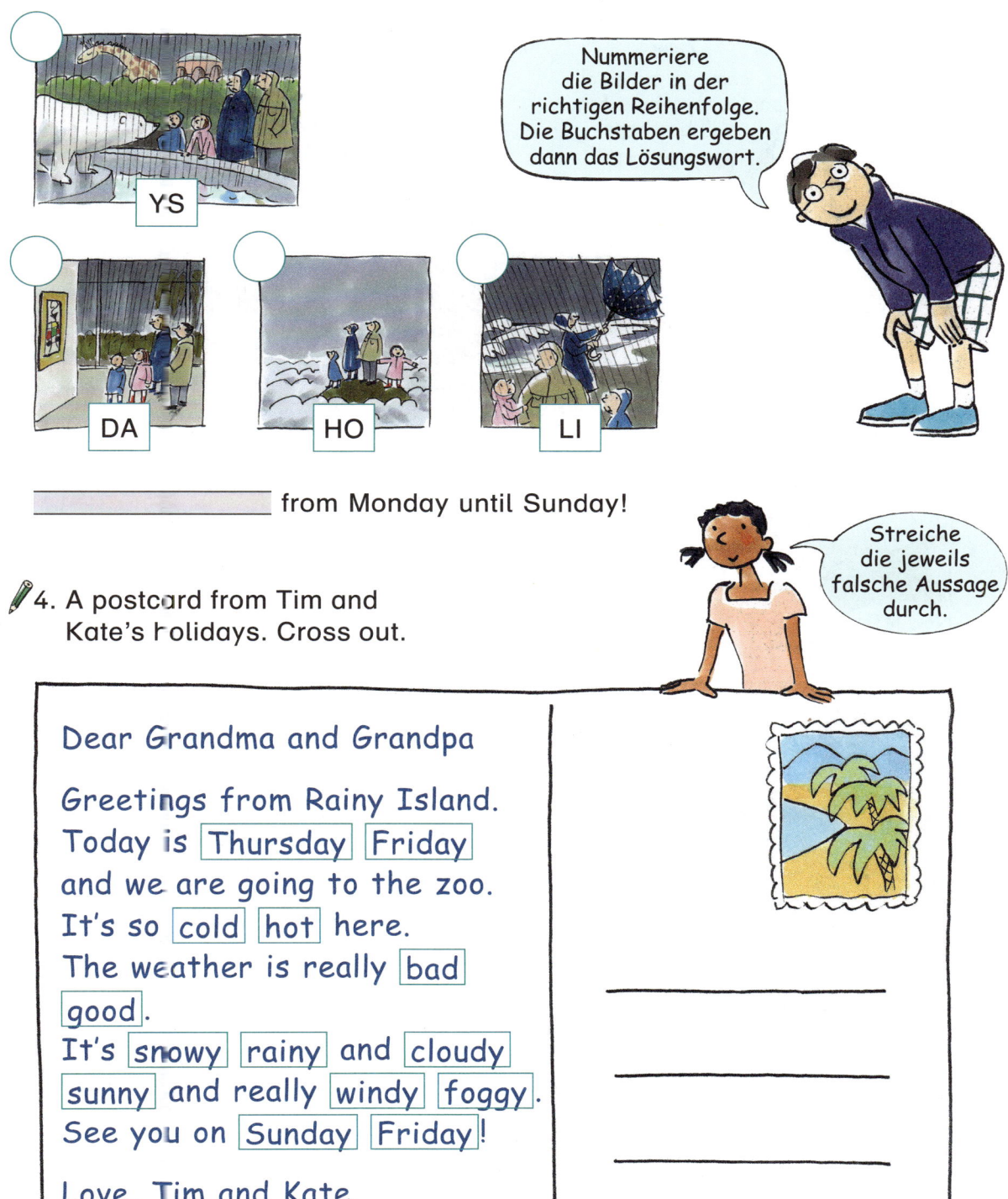

YS

> Nummeriere die Bilder in der richtigen Reihenfolge. Die Buchstaben ergeben dann das Lösungswort.

DA   HO   LI

_____ from Monday until Sunday!

4. A postcard from Tim and Kate's Holidays. Cross out.

> Streiche die jeweils falsche Aussage durch.

Dear Grandma and Grandpa

Greetings from Rainy Island.
Today is Thursday Friday
and we are going to the zoo.
It's so cold hot here.
The weather is really bad
good .
It's snowy rainy and cloudy
sunny and really windy foggy .
See you on Sunday Friday !

Love, Tim and Kate

📕 Comic

Pool party

Koala, come to our pool party. My whole family will be there.

These are my father, my mother, my brother and my sister.

These are my uncle, my aunt, my cousin, my grandpa and my grandma.

And this is my best friend Koala.

Now let's go swimming in the pool.

SPLASH!

But who is who now? Sally, where are you?

Informationen für Eltern und Lehrkräfte

Englisch-Spaß mit Comic-Stars

Aufbau und Gestaltung der Comic-Stars

Comics haben einen hohen Motivationsgrad. Sie erleichtern das Lesen, da sich der Inhalt durch die Bebilderung einfacher erschließen lässt.
Die Comic-Stars führen die Kinder zum ersten Lesen in der Fremdsprache heran und zeigen ihnen, wie viel sie schon selbstständig lesen und verstehen können.

Unterteilt in verschiedene Themenbereiche, können diese unabhängig voneinander gelesen und bearbeitet werden. Jedes Kapitel beginnt mit dem Comic. Daran schließen sich zwei Übungsseiten an. Die erste Seite dient zur Wortschatzwiederholung und -sicherung, während sich die zweite Seite auf den Comic selbst bezieht wobei das Leseverstehen überprüft und der Inhalt reflektiert wird. Die Abschlussseite greift alle Themen nochmals

auf und animiert die Kinder dazu sich ein weiteres Mal mit den Comics zu beschäftigen.
Eindeutige Aufgabenstellungen und Selbstkontrolle durch den Lösungsteil ermöglichen den Kindern eigenständig mit den Comic-Stars zu arbeiten.

Die beiden deutschsprachigen Kinder Anna und Felix unterstützen mit Tipps und Hilfestellungen.

Für jeden gelesenen Comic und für jeden bearbeiteten und kontrollierten Übungsteil dürfen sich die Kinder mit einem Sternchen-Aufkleber belohnen. Für die letzte Seite gibt es zwei weitere Sterne. Als besonderer Anreiz ergeben die Sterne am Ende des Heftes ein Gesamtbild.

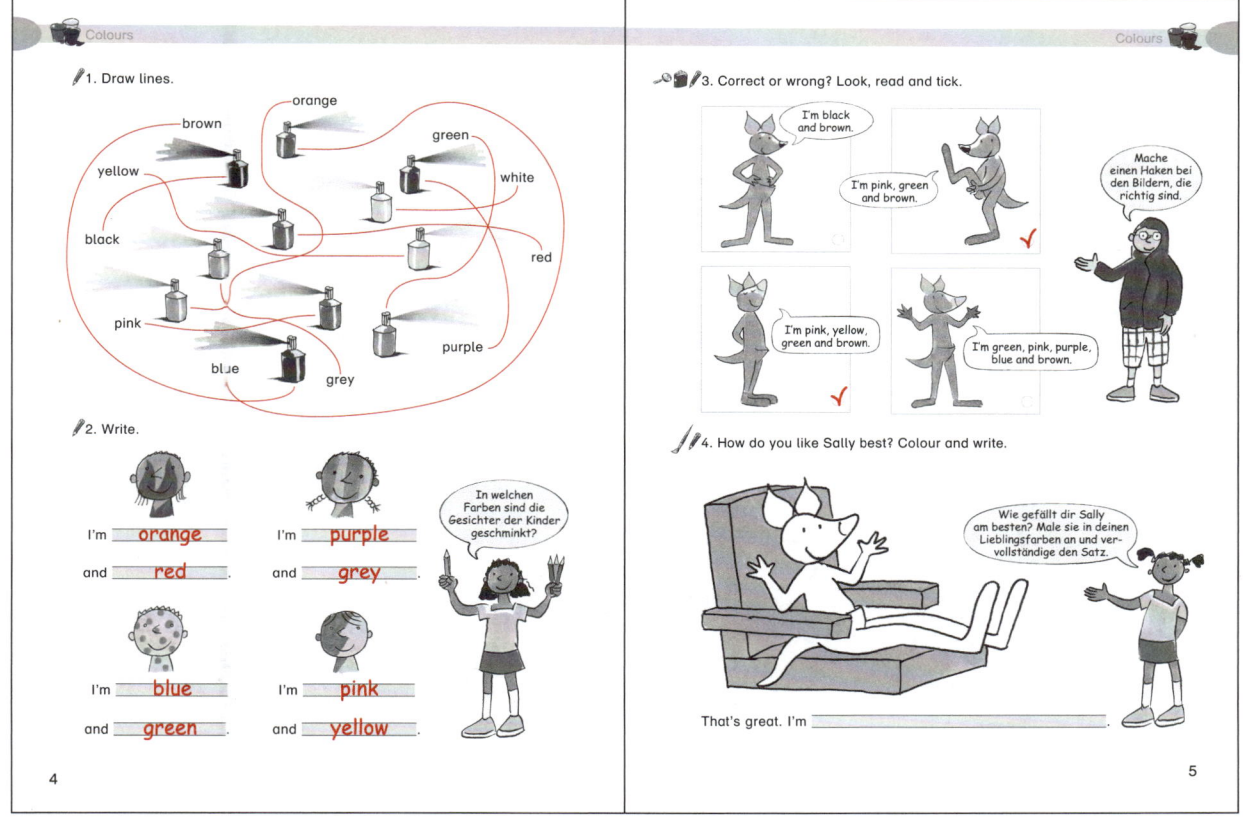

Lösungen

📖 Comic

Who likes lollipops?

We have got **one** loaf of bread, **two** bottles of milk and **three** oranges.

Four bananas.

Five apples.

What's that, Billy? **Six** lollipops? No, Billy!

Seven, eight rolls.

ROLLS

And a package with **nine** chocolate bars.

CHOCOLATE

Oh no, Billy, not again. **Ten** lollipops?

Please, Mum.

Wow! Thank you, Billy. I love lollipops.

6

✏️ 1. Circle the words and write.

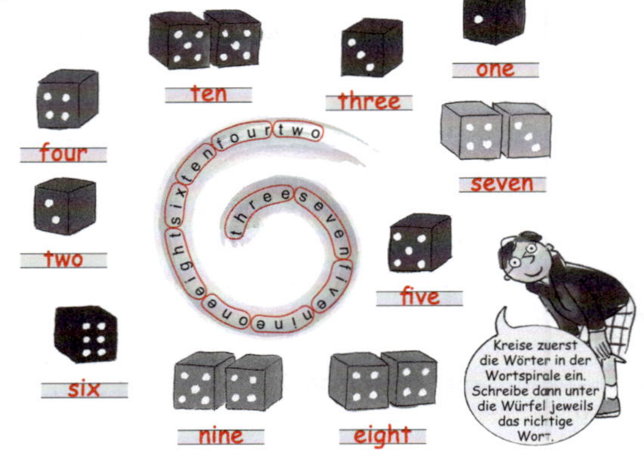

ten

one

three

four

seven

two

five

six

nine

eight

Kreise zuerst die Wörter in der Wortspirale ein. Schreibe dann unter die Würfel jeweils das richtige Wort.

✏️ 2. Join the dots.

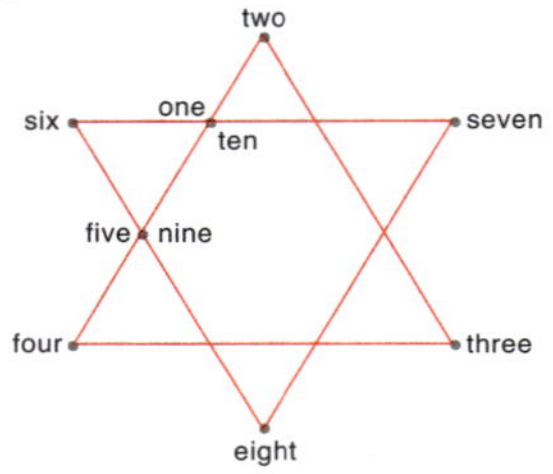

two

six   one   seven
       ten

five   nine

four   three

eight

7

✏️ 3. How many of these things do Billy and his mum buy? Write.

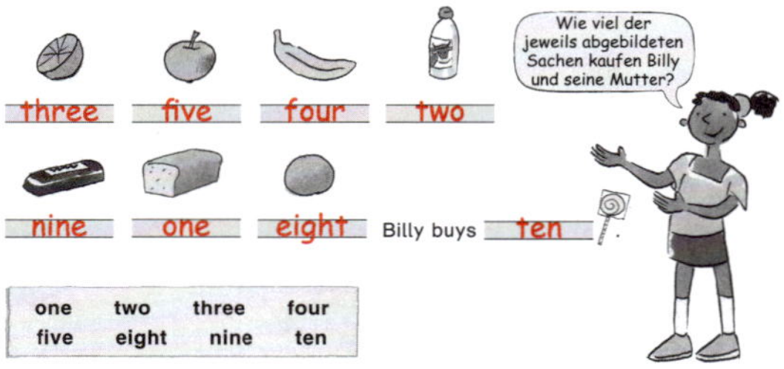

three   five   four   two

nine   one   eight   Billy buys   ten

Wie viel der jeweils abgebildeten Sachen kaufen Billy und seine Mutter?

one	two	three	four
five	eight	nine	ten

✏️ 4. Can you answer the questions? Draw lines and find the word.

Billy and his mum are	at school. (n)
	at home. (z)
	at the supermarket. (f)
They buy	three oranges. (o)
	six oranges. (i)
	nine oranges. (e)
Billy buys	ten lollipops. (u)
	five lollipops. (n)
	eight lollipops. (r)
The lollipops are for	Mum. (e)
	Billy. (o)
	Sally. (r)

The word is: four

One purple, two purple, three purple lollipops,

four purple, five purple, six purple lollipops,

seven purple, eight purple, nine purple lollipops,

ten lollipops for me!

8

📖 Comic

An art lesson

Make an art work of your best friend. Use your coloured pencils, rubber, ruler, glue, water colours and scissors.

That's great. I love art lessons.

coloured pencils   glue
ruler   scissors   water colours
rubber

Can I have your grey pencil, please?

I don't like it.

Can I have your glue, please?

We need more grey paint.

I've got an idea!

That's a great picture of my best friend.

9

At school

1. Look and write.

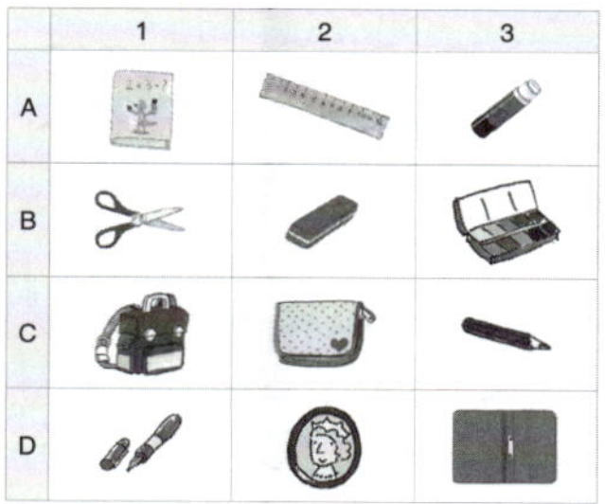

	1	2	3
A			
B			
C			
D			

Suche das Feld in der Tabelle und schreibe das richtige Wort in die Zeile

B2 — rubber
A1 — book
D3 — folder
B3 — water colours
C2 — pencil case
D1 — pen

C3 — pencil
C1 — schoolbag
A3 — glue
B1 — scissors
D2 — picture
A2 — ruler

> scissors   rubber   schoolbag   pencil case
> water colours   picture   folder
> glue   book   pen   ruler   pencil

10

At school

2. Find the word and draw.

Entziffere das Wort und male den Gegenstand.

enp	lurer	berbru
Füller	**Lineal**	**Radiergummi**

eulg	srosciss	cinpel
Klebstoff	**Schere**	**Bleistift**

3. What do Sally and Koala need for their art lesson? Tick the correct answers.

- ◯ pen
- ✓ coloured pencils
- ◯ book
- ✓ rubber
- ✓ ruler
- ◯ folder
- ✓ water colours
- ◯ pencil case
- ✓ scissors
- ✓ glue

4. Number the pictures in the correct order. Draw lines.

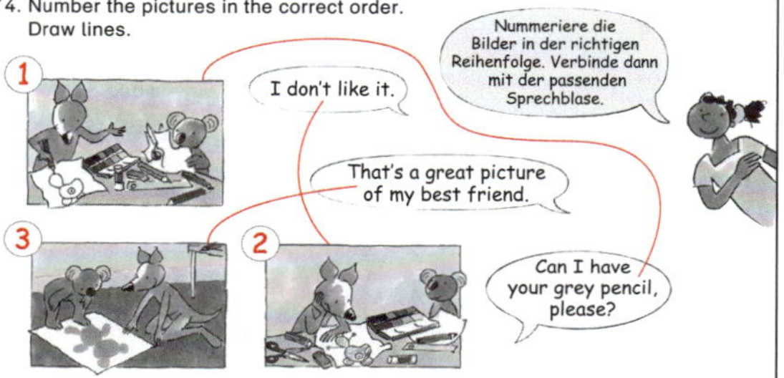

Nummeriere die Bilder in der richtigen Reihenfolge. Verbinde dann mit der passenden Sprechblase.

1 — I don't like it.

That's a great picture of my best friend.

3   2 — Can I have your grey pencil, please?

11

Body and feelings

🗨 Comic

A walk at night

Let's start our night walk.

Lilly, are you scared?

Yes, give me your hand.

Ouch! My head!

Shhh! What is it? I can see eyes.

Oh, look at the long ears! It's only a little rabbit.

And I'm really hungry now.

My feet hurt.

Let's go back.

I'm tired.

A great walk. I'm so happy it was only a rabbit.

Yummy, sausages!

12

Body and feelings

1. Write and draw.

head
eye(s)   nose
ear(s)   mouth
arm(s)   hand(s)
leg(s)
foot/feet

> head   eyes   mouth   ears   nose
> legs   arms   hands   foot/feet

Ergänze das Gesicht und beschrifte die Körperteile.

2. How do they feel? Do the crossword.

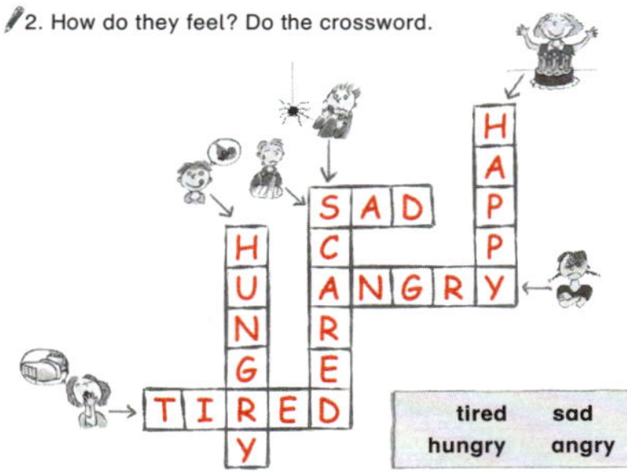

```
            H
      S A D A
    H   C   P
    U A N G R Y
    N   A
    G   R
    R   E
T I R E D
    Y   D
```

> tired   sad   happy
> hungry   angry   scared

13

Lösungen

3. Look at the comic and complete the sentences. Draw lines.

Lilly, are you ___scared___?

Ouch! My ___head___!

I can see ___eyes___.

Oh, look at the long ___ears___!

I'm really ___hungry___ now.

I'm so ___happy___ it was only a rabbit.

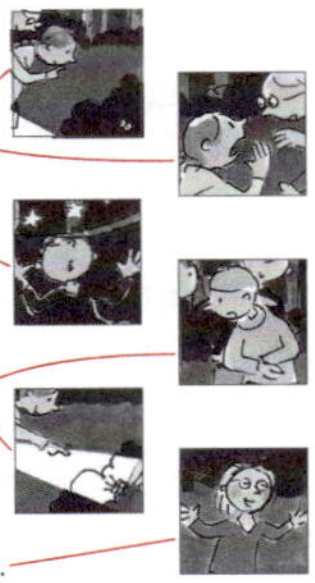

4. Draw lines and circle the correct letters.
Find out, how the children feel.

	Is Lilly happy?	Yes, she is. (sc) No, she isn't. (hu)
	Is the boy angry?	Yes, he is. (ar) No, he isn't. (ng)
	Is the girl tired?	Yes, she is. (ry) No, she isn't. (ed)

The children are very ___hungry___.

14

Comic

Money for new toys

15

---

1. Where are the toys? Look and write.

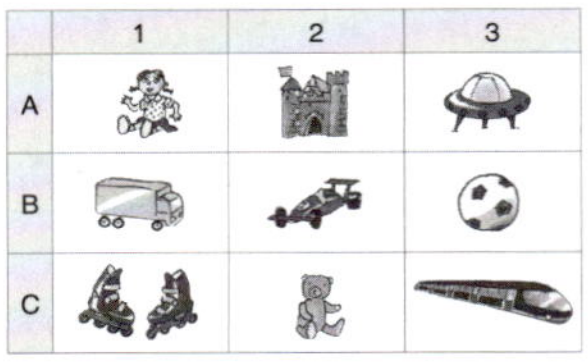

Schreibe zuerst auf, in welchem Feld sich jeweils der Gegenstand befindet. Trage unten dann die Wörter richtig ein.

In which square...

is the **ball**? ___B3___

is the **lorry**? ___B1___　　is the **doll**? ___A1___

is the **castle**? ___A2___　　is the **racing car**? ___B2___

is the **spaceship**? ___A3___　　are the **inline skates**? ___C1___

is the **train**? ___C3___　　is the **teddy bear**? ___C2___

teddy bear 　　doll 　　castle

racing car 　　train 　　inline skates

ball 　　spaceship 　　lorry

16

2. Match the sentences with the correct person. Draw lines.

We don't need a new doll and a new racing car.

Let's do a flea market and sell some toys.

How much are the castle and the teddy bear?

You have so many toys. I'm not buying anything else for you.

How much are the ball and the train?

We need money for the doll and the racing car.

3. What's wrong in the pictures? Write.

Schreibe auf was fehlt und streiche im Bild durch, was zu viel ist.

The ___doll___ is missing.

The ___ball___ and the ___train___ are ___missing___.

The ___castle___ and the ___teddy bear___ are ___missing___.

17

Clothes

Comic

Sally's patchwork dress

18

✏ 1. What can you see? Write.

trousers

dress

pullover

blouse

T-shirt

shoes

skirt

anorak

| T-shirt | anorak | skirt | pullover | trousers |
| blouse | dress | shoes | | |

✏ 2. Do the clothes fit? Draw lines and write.

The **pullover** is **too small** .

The **skirt** is **just right** .

The **shoes** are **too big** .

The **blouse** is **too old** .

19

Clothes

✏ 3. Tick the correct answer.

Sally wants to go	to school.	○
	shopping.	○
	to Tina's birthday party.	✓
Sally wants	a dress.	✓
	a coat.	○
	a pair of trousers.	○
The red skirt is	too small.	○
	too old.	○
	too big.	✓
Sally	likes her new dress.	✓
	doesn't like her new dress.	○
	likes her old dress.	○

1₂3 4. Number the sentences in the correct order.

2 I don't know what to wear to the party.

7 I'm off to Tina's party now. Thank you, Mummy, you are great.

6 Mummy, can you help me, please?

4 I've got an idea!

3 The yellow dress is too small, the red skirt is too big and the blue blouse is too old.

1 Great! Tina wants me to come to her birthday party.

5 That looks nice. I like my new dress.

20

Weather and days

Comic

Rainy holidays

21

Lösungen

1. What's the weather like? Write.

It's **windy** and **cloudy**.

It's **rainy** and **foggy**.

It's **sunny** and **hot**.

It's **snowy** and **cold**.

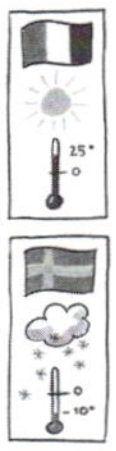

sunny	rainy	snowy	cloudy	foggy
	windy	cold	hot	

2. Find the words and number in the correct order.

③ Wednesday   ⑥ Saturday

② Tuesday   ① Monday

⑤ Friday   ④ Thursday

⑦ Sunday

Sunday	Friday	Monday	Saturday
Thursday	Tuesday	Wednesday	

22

3. Number the pictures in the correct order. Find the word.

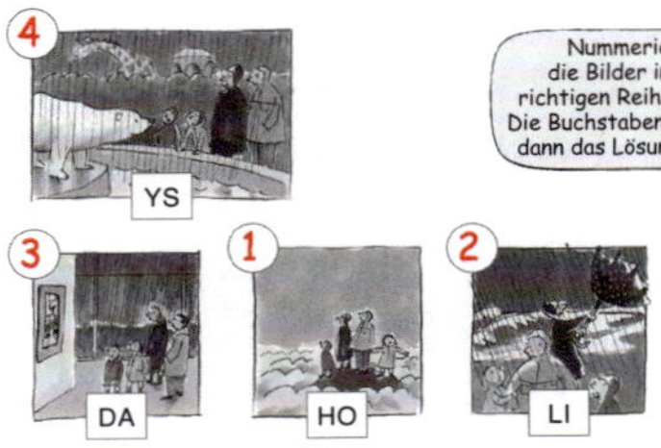

④ YS   ③ DA   ① HO   ② LI

Nummeriere die Bilder in der richtigen Reihenfolge. Die Buchstaben ergeben dann das Lösungswort.

Holidays from Monday until Sunday!

4. A postcard from Tim and Kate's holidays. Cross out.

Streiche die jeweils falsche Aussage durch.

Dear Grandma and Grandpa

Greetings from Rainy Island.
Today is ~~Thursday~~ Friday
and we are going to the zoo.
It's so ~~cold~~ ~~hot~~ here.
The weather is really bad
~~good~~.
It's ~~snowy~~ rainy and cloudy
~~sunny~~ and really ~~windy~~ foggy.
See you on Sunday ~~Friday~~!

Love, Tim and Kate

23

Comic

Pool party

Koala, come to our pool party. My whole family will be there.

These are my father, my mother, my brother and my sister.

These are my uncle, my aunt, my cousin, my grandpa and my grandma.

And this is my best friend Koala.

Now let's go swimming in the pool.

SPLASH!

But who is who now? Sally, where are you?

24

1. Who is it? Write.

mother   **grandfather**   **father**

brother   **grandmother**   **sister**

aunt   **cousin**   **uncle**

2. Different families. Write.

Schau genau hin und ergänze dann die Sätze.

I live with my father, my **mother** and my **brother**.

I live with my **mother**, my **grandmother** and my **grandfather**.

I live with my **father**, my **mother**, my **sister**, my uncle, my **aunt** and my **cousin**.

25

Family and friends

3. Draw lines.

These are my uncle, my aunt, my cousin, my grandpa and my grandma.

Koala, come to our pool party.

Ordne die Sprechblase dem richtigen Bild zu.

These are my father, my mother, my brother and my sister.

And this is my best friend Koala.

4. Who is it? Read, look and write.

Who is it? He's wearing green trousers.

That's my **uncle**.

Who is it? She's wearing a pink dress.

That's my **mother**.

Who is it? He's wearing a yellow T-Shirt.

That's my **grandfather**.

Who is it? She's wearing a purple skirt.

That's my **sister**.

Schau dir den Comic nochmal genau an und ergänze dann die Sätze.

26

Drinks

Comic

A game with drinks

Come on, let's play a game.

What is it, Jack?

Ah, that's orange juice.

One is water and one is lemonade.

Ew! That tastes bitter! That's coffee! Now it's your turn!

What is it, Betty?

Yummy, it's my favourite drink, hot chocolate.

Mmmm, one is milk. I like it. The other one is coke.

Now you get my favourite drink.

I'm mixing everything together.

Do you like my special drink?

27

Drinks

1. What is it? Write.

milk   coke   coffee

apple juice   orange juice

hot chocolate   tea

water   lemonade

apple juice   milk   coke   lemonade   tea
hot chocolate   coffee   water   orange juice

2. Read and write.

It's cold, bubbly and made from lemons. It's **lemonade**.

It's cold, brown and sweet. Children like it. It's **coke**.

It's cold. It's made from apples. It's **apple juice**.

You can drink it warm or cold. It's white and from a cow.

It's **milk**.

It's hot, brown and sweet. You make it with milk.

It's **hot chocolate**.

28

Drinks

3. Cross out.

Jack ~~likes~~ doesn't like coffee.

Coffee tastes bitter ~~sweet~~.

Betty likes ~~doesn't like~~ milk.

Betty's favourite drink is ~~coke~~ hot chocolate.

Streiche jeweils die falsche Aussage durch.

4. Look at the comic and write.

Jack

orange juice, water, lemonade, coffee

Betty

hot chocolate, milk, coke, special drink

Schreibe auf, welche Getränke Jack und welche Betty probiert hat.

What's your favourite drink?

My favourite drink is

29

Comic

Sally's special breakfast

RINGGG!

Oh, I'm sooooo tired.

Good morning, Mum.

Good morning, Sally. Would you like milk, orange juice or tea? And would you like a roll with butter or bread with ham?

Just hot chocolate.

Oh, no! I put strawberry jam into the milk.

I'll try it.

Yummy! It's strawberry-jam milk.

Now, I'm ready for school!

Goodbye, Mum. And thank you for the great breakfast.

Oh, Sally!

---

1. Find the words and draw lines.

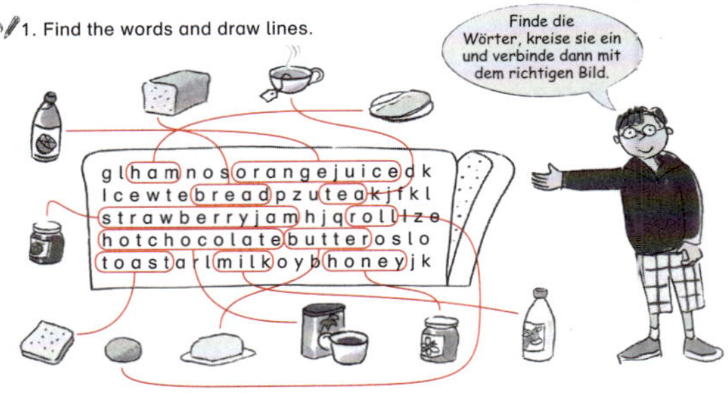

Finde die Wörter, kreise sie ein und verbinde dann mit dem richtigen Bild.

```
g l h a m n o s o r a n g e j u i c e d k
l c e w t e b r e a d p z u t e a k j f k l
s t r a w b e r r y j a m h j q r o l l t z e
h o t c h o c o l a t e b u t t e r o s l o
t o a s t a r l m i l k o y b h o n e y j k
```

2. What do they like for breakfast? Trace the lines and write.

Lucy   Ben   Tom

Lucy likes __tea__ and **bread** with **ham**.

Ben likes __orange juice__ and __toast__

with __butter__.

Tom likes __milk__ and a __roll__

with __strawberry jam__.

---

3. Read and tick the correct answer.

Sally says:	Hello, Mum.	○
	Good morning, Mum.	✓
	Good night, Mum.	○
Sally wants …	milk	○	for breakfast.
	orange juice	○	
	hot chocolate	✓	
Sally puts …	chocolate	○	into her milk.
	strawberry jam	✓	
	ham	○	
Does Sally like strawberry milk?	Yes, she does.	✓
	No, she doesn't.	○

4. Sally's crazy breakfast. Look and write.

On Monday Sally has strawberry-jam milk.

On Tuesday Sally has an
orange-juice roll.

On Wednesday Sally has
__hot-chocolate tea__

But on Saturday and Sunday, there's no school – and I'm not tired.

On Thursday Sally has
__orange-juice milk__

On Friday Sally has
__hot-chocolate bread__

Comic

Eating a rainbow

Lucy, eat some fruit. It's good for you.

I don't like to eat what's good for me.

Strawberries are red – and cherries are red, too.

Oranges are orange.

Lemons are yellow – and bananas are yellow, too.

Apples are green – and pears are green, too.

Plums are purple.

Well, grapes are blue.

Good girl, you're eating fruit.

I'm not eating fruit, Mummy, I'm eating a rainbow.

Fruit

1. Draw lines.

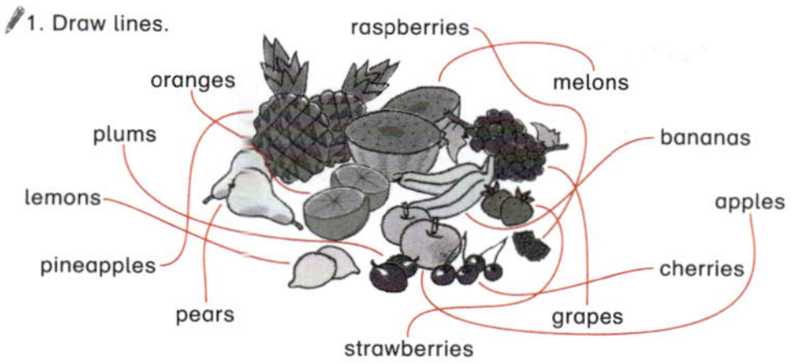

raspberries
oranges
melons
plums
bananas
lemons
apples
pineapples
cherries
pears
grapes
strawberries

2. What can you see n the squares? Write.

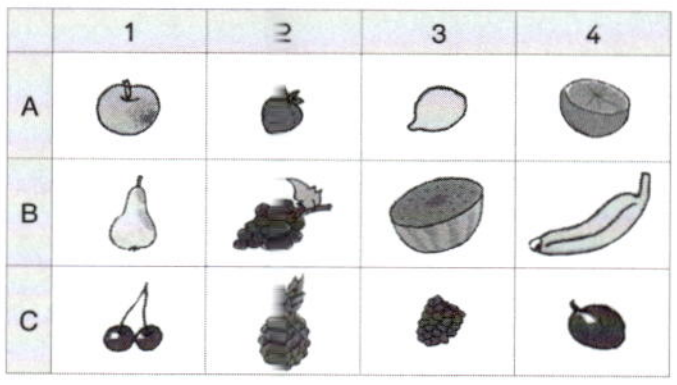

	1	2	3	4
A				
B				
C				

apple
banana
cherries
grapes
lemon
melon
orange
pear
pineapple
plum
strawberry
raspberry

A1 **apple**   B1 **pear**

B4 **banana**   C4 **plum**

C1 **cherries**   A4 **orange**

B2 **grapes**   C2 **pineapple**

A3 **lemon**   A2 **strawberry**

B3 **melon**   C3 **raspberry**

34

Fruit

3. Look at the comic and write.

__Strawberries__ and __cherries__ are red.

__Apples__ and __pears__ are green.

__Lemons__ and __bananas__ are yellow.

__Plums__ are purple.

__Oranges__ are orange.

__Grapes__ are blue.

4. Correct or wrong?
Circle the letters and you will find a fruit. Draw it.

	correct	wrong
Lucy likes to eat fruit.	P	(A)
Bananas are red.	L	(P)
Lemons are yellow.	(P)	U
Cherries are big.	M	(L)
Lucy eats a rainbow of fruit.	(E)	S

APPLE

35

Pets

Comic

All my pets

I have only got one dog. I'd like to have another dog and a budgie.

Make your wishes.

I would also like to have a guinea pig, a mouse, a rabbit and a hamster.

I'm so happy. I have got lots of pets.

And I'd like to have a cat, and a fish and a tortoise.

Oh no!

Oh, good, it was only a dream. One pet is enough for me.

36

Pets

1. What do you see in the squares? Look and write.

	1	2	3
A			
B			
C			

budgie   tortoise
fish   dog
rabbit   mouse
cat   hamster
guinea pig

B1: It's a __rabbit__.   A1: __It's a fish__.

C3: It's a __tortoise__.   C1: __It's a budgie__.

C2: __It's a guinea pig__.   B3: __It's a cat__.

A3: __It's a mouse__.   A2: __It's a hamster__.

B2: __It's a dog__.

2. Whose is it? Write.

__tortoise__   __budgie__

__dog__   __hamster__

__fish__

__cat__

Zu welchem Tier gehört welcher Gegenstand? Schreibe auf.

37

Lösungen

3. Look at the comic. Number the pets in the correct order.

7 | 8 | 6
4 | 1 | 5
3 | 2 | 9

4. Which animals are missing? Write.

The **rabbit**, the **budgie**, the **fish** and the **hamster** are missing.

The **cat**, the **tortoise** and the **mouse** are missing.

38

Comic

Fun outside

Sally, it stopped raining! Please go and play outside.

Goodbye, Mum. · Goodbye, Sally.

Climbing a tree is great.

SCRATCH!

Thank you, bird, for this nice feather.

I love catching frogs in the pond.

Oh no, SALLY!!!

Hello, Mum, I love playing outside.

I'm picking some flowers for Mum.

39

1. Find the words and draw lines.

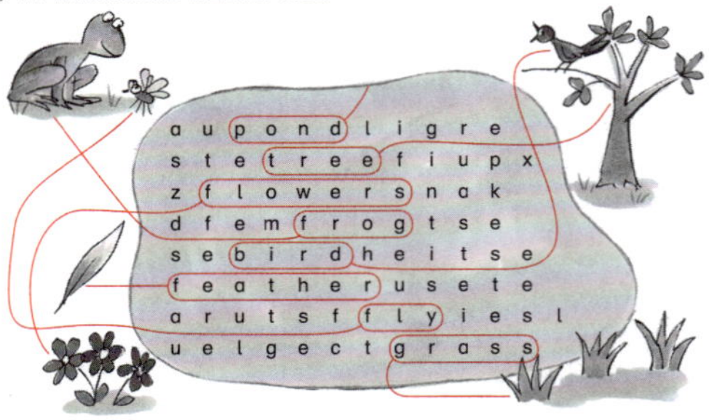

```
a u p o n d l i g r e
s t e t r e e f i u p x
z f l o w e r s n a k
d f e m f r o g t s e
s e b i r d h e i t s e
f e a t h e r u s e t e
a r u t s f f l y i e s l
u e l g e c t g r a s s
```

grass   pond   tree   fly   frog
feather   flowers   bird

2. Find out who it is. Look, read and write.

Mary   **Andy**   **Lilly**   **Sam**

Andy is catching a **fly**.

Lilly is picking **flowers**.

Sam is climbing a **tree**.

Mary is jumping like a **frog**.

Vervollständige zunächst die Sätze. Ordne dann die Namen der Kinder dem passenden Bild zu.

40

3. Number the sentences in the correct order. Match them with the correct picture.

Nummeriere die Sätze in der richtigen Reihenfolge und ordne sie dem passenden Bild zu.

4 | 2
3
1

2 — Sally has got a feather.

1 — Sally is climbing a tree.

4 — Sally is picking flowers for her mum.

3 — Sally is catching a frog in the pond.

4. What does Sally like? Draw lines and circle the correct letter. Who's Sally's new friend?

Sally likes catching frogs	in the pond. (f) / in the grass. (b)
Sally likes picking flowers	for her sister. (i) / for her mum. (r)
Sally likes climbing	a tree. (o) / a house. (r)
Sally likes	colours. (d) / feathers. (g)

Sally's new friend is a **frog**.

41

Farm animals

Comic

I want to ride a ...

Farm animals

1. Guess the farm animal. Write.

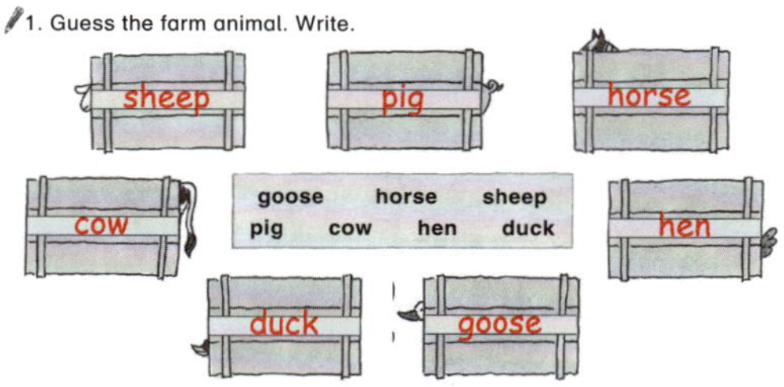

sheep | pig | horse

cow

goose   horse   sheep
pig   cow   hen   duck

hen

duck | goose

2. What animal is it? Read and write.

It likes carrots and says neigh-neigh. It's a **horse**.

It's pink and says oink-oink. It's a **pig**.

It's big and gives milk. It's a **cow**.

It says cluck-cluck and lays eggs. It's a **hen**.

It can swim and says quak-quak. It's a **duck**.

It's bigger than a duck. It says honk-honk. It's a **goose**.

It eats grass and says baa-baa. It's a **sheep**.

42 | 43

Farm animals

3. Number the pictures in the correct order.

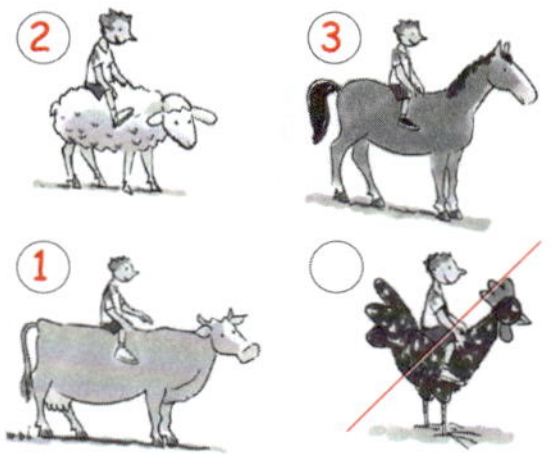

Achtung! Schau genau hin! Ein Bild musst du durchstreichen.

4. Correct or wrong? Tick.

	correct	wrong
The farmer is riding a pig.		✓
The boy wants to ride a cow.	✓	
The boy wants to feed a sheep.		✓
The boy wants to ride a goose.		✓
The hens, the ducks and the goose are laughing at the boy.	✓	

Great Britain

Comic

Hide-and-seek in London

44 | 45

Lösungen

1. Do the crossword.

```
              T O W E R B R I D G E
B U C K I N G H A M P A L A C E
      B I G B E N
              Q
L O N D O N E Y E
      U N I O N J A C K
```

_____The Queen_____ lives at Buckingham Palace.

| Buckingham Palace | London Eye | Big Ben |
| Union Jack | the Queen | Tower Bridge |

2. Cross out.

~~The Union Jack~~ The London Eye is a big 🎡.

~~The London Eye~~ Big Ben is a 🔔.

Buckingham Palace ~~Tower Bridge~~ is the home of the 👑.

The Union Jack ~~Big Ben~~ is the 🏴 of Great Britain.

46

3. Correct or wrong? Circle the letters and write down the word.

	correct	wrong
Sally and Koala are in New York.	C	(F)
Sally and Koala play hide-and-seek.	(L)	B
Sally and Koala visit the Queen.	N	(A)
Sally and Koala go by bus.	(G)	E

FLAG

4. Look and write.

Schau dir nochmal den Comic an. Schreibe auf, wer von beiden sich bei der abgebildeten Sehenswürdigkeit versteckt hat. Schreibe auch den Namen der Sehenswürdigkeit auf.

__Sally__ is on the ____London Eye____

__Koala__ is at ____Buckingham Palace____

__Koala__ is at ____Tower Bridge____.

47

Look at the comics again. Find the correct answer and write down the letter. What can you read?

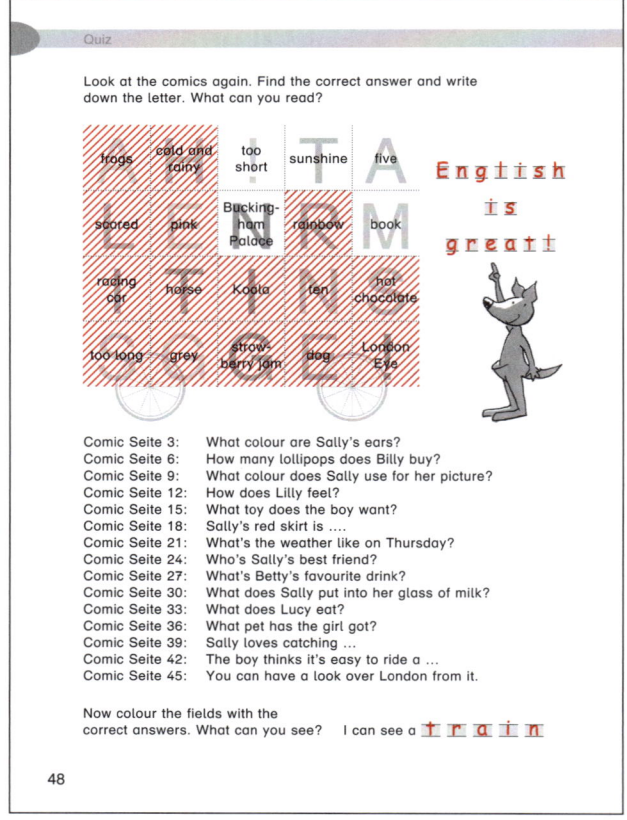

English is great!

frogs	cold and rainy	too short	sunshine	five
scared	pink	Buckingham Palace	rainbow	book
racing car	horse	Koala	ten	hot chocolate
too long	grey	strawberry jam	dog	London Eye

Comic Seite 3: What colour are Sally's ears?
Comic Seite 6: How many lollipops does Billy buy?
Comic Seite 9: What colour does Sally use for her picture?
Comic Seite 12: How does Lilly feel?
Comic Seite 15: What toy does the boy want?
Comic Seite 18: Sally's red skirt is ....
Comic Seite 21: What's the weather like on Thursday?
Comic Seite 24: Who's Sally's best friend?
Comic Seite 27: What's Betty's favourite drink?
Comic Seite 30: What does Sally put into her glass of milk?
Comic Seite 33: What does Lucy eat?
Comic Seite 36: What pet has the girl got?
Comic Seite 39: Sally loves catching ...
Comic Seite 42: The boy thinks it's easy to ride a ...
Comic Seite 45: You can have a look over London from it.

Now colour the fields with the
correct answers. What can you see?   I can see a **train**

48

Hier hast du Platz zum Üben

✏️ 1. Who is it? Write.

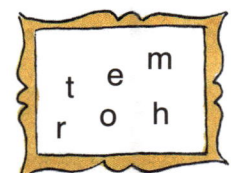

_____

_____

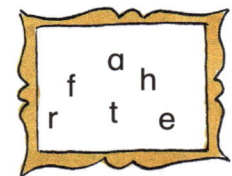

_____

_____

_____

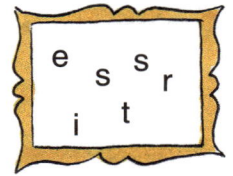

_____

_____

_____

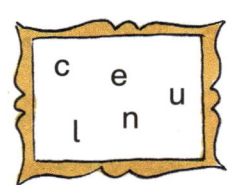

_____

✏️ 2. Different families. Write.

I live with my father, my _____ and

my _____ .

I live with my _____ , my

_____ and my _____ .

I live with my _____ , my _____ ,

my _____ , my uncle, my _____

and my _____ .

Schau genau hin und ergänze dann die Sätze.

25

3. Draw lines.

These are my uncle, my aunt, my cousin, my grandpa and my grandma.

Koala, come to our pool party.

Ordne die Sprechblase dem richtigen Bild zu.

These are my father, my mother, my brother and my sister.

And this is my best friend Koala.

4. Who is it? Read, look and write.

 Who is it? He's wearing green trousers.

 That's my _____.

 Who is it? She's wearing a pink dress.

 That's my _____.

 Who is it? He's wearing a yellow T-Shirt.

 That's my _____.

 Who is it? She's wearing a purple skirt.

 That's my _____.

Schau dir den Comic nochmal genau an und ergänze dann die Sätze.

📕 Comic

A game with drinks

1. What is it? Write.

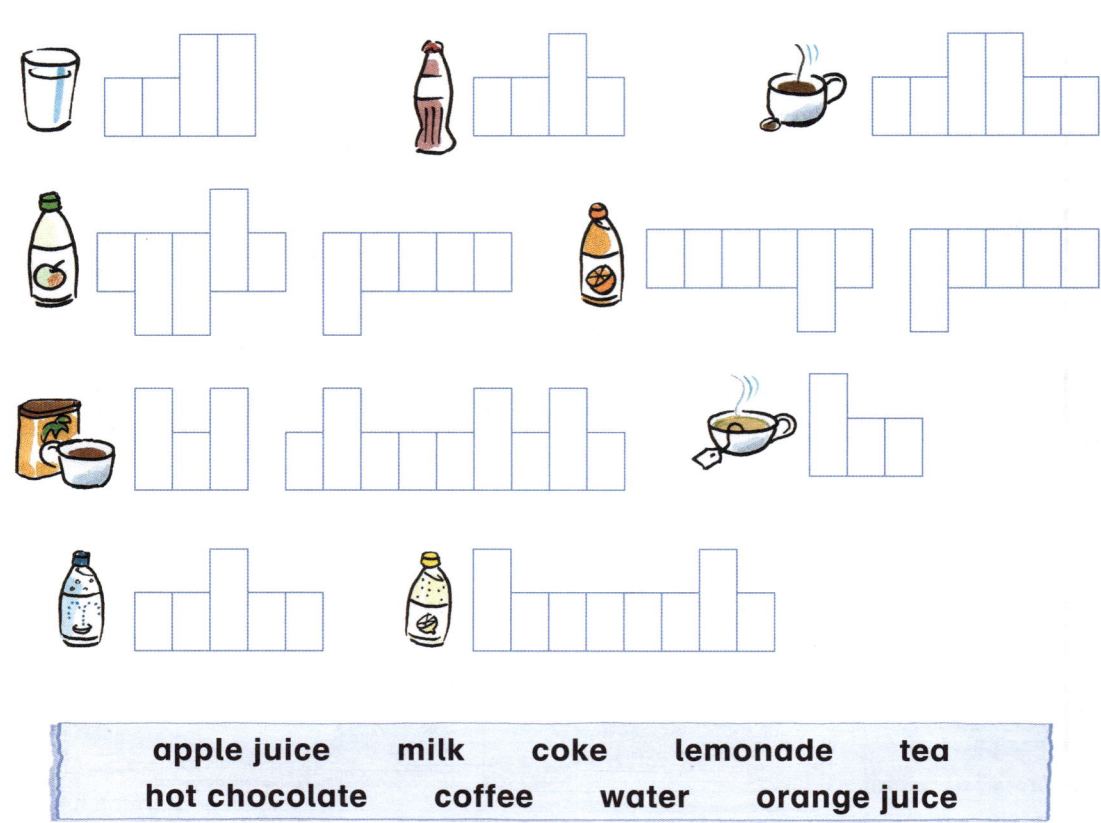

| apple juice | milk | coke | lemonade | tea |
| hot chocolate | coffee | water | orange juice | |

2. Read and write.

It's cold, bubbly and made from lemons. It's _____.

It's cold, brown and sweet. Children like it. It's _____.

It's cold. It's made from apples. It's _____.

You can drink it warm or cold. It's white and from a cow.

It's _____.

It's hot, brown and sweet. You make it with milk.

It's _____.

3. Cross out.

Jack likes | doesn't like coffee.

Coffee tastes bitter | sweet .

Betty likes | doesn't like milk.

Betty's favourite drink is coke | hot chocolate .

Streiche jeweils die falsche Aussage durch.

4. Look at the comic and write.

Jack

Schreibe auf, welche Getränke Jack und welche Betty probiert hat.

Betty

What's your favourite drink?

My favourite drink is _____ .

📕 Comic

Sally's special breakfast

1. Find the words and draw lines.

Finde die Wörter, kreise sie ein und verbinde dann mit dem richtigen Bild.

```
g l h a m n o s o r a n g e j u i c e d k
l c e w t e b r e a d p z u t e a k j f k l
s t r a w b e r r y j a m h j q r o l l l z e
h o t c h o c o l a t e b u t t e r o s l o
t o a s t a r l m i l k o y b h o n e y j k
```

2. What do they like for breakfast? Trace the lines and write.

Lucy   Ben   Tom

Lucy likes _____ and **bread** with **ham**.

Ben likes _____ and _____

with _____.

Tom likes _____ and a _____

with _____.

31

3. Read and tick the correct answer.

Sally says:	Hello, Mum. ○ Good morning, Mum. ○ Good night, Mum. ○	
Sally wants …	milk ○ orange juice ○ hot chocolate ○	for breakfast.
Sally puts …	chocolate ○ strawberry jam ○ ham ○	into her milk.
Does Sally like strawberry milk?	Yes, she does. ○ No, she doesn't. ○	

4. Sally's crazy breakfast. Look and write.

On Monday Sally has strawberry-jam milk.

On Tuesday Sally has an
orange-juice roll.

On Wednesday Sally has

_____.

On Thursday Sally has

_____.

> But on Saturday and Sunday, there's no school – and I'm not tired.

On Friday Sally has

_____.

Comic

Eating a rainbow

Lucy, eat some fruit. It's good for you.

I don'– like to eat what's good for me.

Strawberries are red – and cherries are red, too.

Oranges are orange.

Lemons are yellow – and bananas are yellow, too.

Apples are green – and pears are green, too.

Well, grapes are blue.

Plums are purple.

Good girl, you're eating fruit.

I'm not eating fruit, Mummy, I'm eating a rainbow.

33

✏ 1. Draw lines.

raspberries

oranges   melons

plums   bananas

lemons   apples

pineapples   cherries

pears   grapes

strawberries

✏ 2. What can you see in the squares? Write.

	1	2	3	4
A	 🍎	 🍓	 🍋	 🍊
B	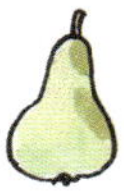 🍐	 🍇	 🍉	 🍌
C	 🍒	 🍍	 raspberry	 plum

apple
banana
cherries
grapes
lemon
melon
orange
pear
pineapple
plum
strawberry
raspberry

A1 ☐☐☐☐☐   B1 ☐☐☐☐

B4 ☐☐☐☐☐☐   C4 ☐☐☐☐

C1 ☐☐☐☐☐☐☐   A4 ☐☐☐☐☐☐

B2 ☐☐☐☐☐☐   C2 ☐☐☐☐☐☐☐☐

A3 ☐☐☐☐☐   A2 ☐☐☐☐☐☐☐☐☐☐

B3 ☐☐☐☐☐   C3 ☐☐☐☐☐☐☐☐☐

3. Look at the comic and write.

_____ and _____ are red.

_____ and _____ are green.

_____ and _____ are yellow.

_____ are purple.

_____ are orange.

_____ are blue.

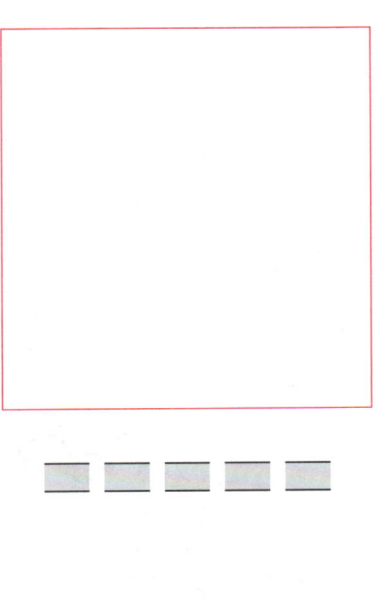

4. Correct or wrong?
Circle the letters and you will find a fruit. Draw it.

	correct	wrong
Lucy likes to eat fruit.	P	A
Bananas are red.	L	P
Lemons are yellow.	P	U
Cherries are big.	M	L
Lucy eats a rainbow of fruit.	E	S

____ ____ ____ ____ ____

📕 Comic

All my pets

1. What do you see in the squares? Look and write.

	1	2	3
A			
B			
C			

budgie   tortoise
fish   dog
rabbit   mouse
cat   hamster
guinea pig

B1: It's a _____.   A1: _____.

C3: It's a _____.   C1: _____.

C2: _____.   B3: _____.

A3: _____.   A2: _____.

B2: _____.

2. Whose is it? Write.

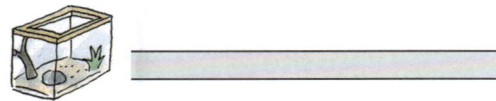

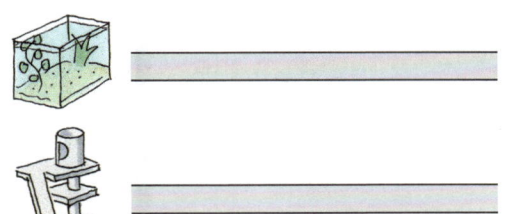

Zu welchem Tier gehört welcher Gegenstand? Schreibe auf.

37

3. Look at the comic. Number the pets in the correct order.

4. Which animals are missing? Write.

The _____, the

_____, the _____

and the _____ are missing.

The _____, the

_____ and the

_____ are missing.

📕 Comic

Fun outside

1. Find the words and draw lines.

```
a  u  p  o  n  d  l  i  g  r  e
s  t  e  t  r  e  e  f  i  u  p  x
z  f  l  o  w  e  r  s  n  a  k
d  f  e  m  f  r  o  g  t  s  e
s  e  b  i  r  d  h  e  i  t  s  e
f  e  a  t  h  e  r  u  s  e  t  e
a  r  u  t  s  f  f  l  y  i  e  s  l
u  e  l  g  e  c  t  g  r  a  s  s
```

grass	pond	tree	fly	frog
	feather	flowers	bird	

2. Find out who it is. Look, read and write.

_____   _____   _____   _____

Andy is catching a _____.

Lilly is picking _____.

Sam is climbing a _____.

Mary is jumping like a _____.

> Ver-
> vollständige
> zunächst die
> Sätze. Ordne dann
> die Namen der
> Kinder dem
> passenden
> Bild zu.

3. Number the sentences in the correct order.
Match them with the correct picture.

SCRATCH!

Nummeriere die Sätze in der richtigen Reihenfolge und ordne sie dem passenden Bild zu.

Sally has got a feather.

Sally is climbing a tree.

Sally is picking flowers for her mum.

Sally is catching a frog in the pond.

4. What does Sally like? Draw lines and circle the correct letter.
Who's Sally's new friend?

Sally likes catching frogs	in the pond. (f) in the grass. (b)
Sally likes picking flowers	for her sister. (i) for her mum. (r)
Sally likes climbing	a tree. (o) a house. (r)
Sally likes	colours. (d) feathers. (g)

Sally's new friend is a ______________ .

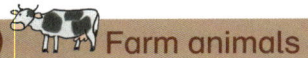

 Comic

I want to ride a ...

1. Guess the farm animal. Write.

goose   horse   sheep
pig   cow   hen   duck

2. What animal is it? Read and write.

It likes carrots and says neigh-neigh. It's a ▢▢▢▢▢ .

It's pink and says oink-oink. It's a ▢▢▢ .

It's big and gives milk. It's a ▢▢▢ .

It says cluck-cluck and lays eggs. It's a ▢▢▢ .

It can swim and says quak-quak. It's a ▢▢▢▢ .

It's bigger than a duck. It says honk-honk. It's a ▢▢▢▢▢ .

It eats grass and says baa-baa. It's a ▢▢▢▢▢ .

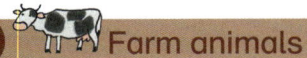
1₂3 3. Number the pictures in the correct order.

Achtung!
Schau genau hin!
Ein Bild musst du
durchstreichen.

4. Correct or wrong? Tick.

	correct	wrong
The farmer is riding a pig.	○	○
The boy wants to ride a cow.	○	○
The boy wants to feed a sheep.	○	○
The boy wants to ride a goose.	○	○
The hens, the ducks and the goose are laughing at the boy.	○	○

📕 Comic

Hide-and-seek in London

1. Do the crossword.

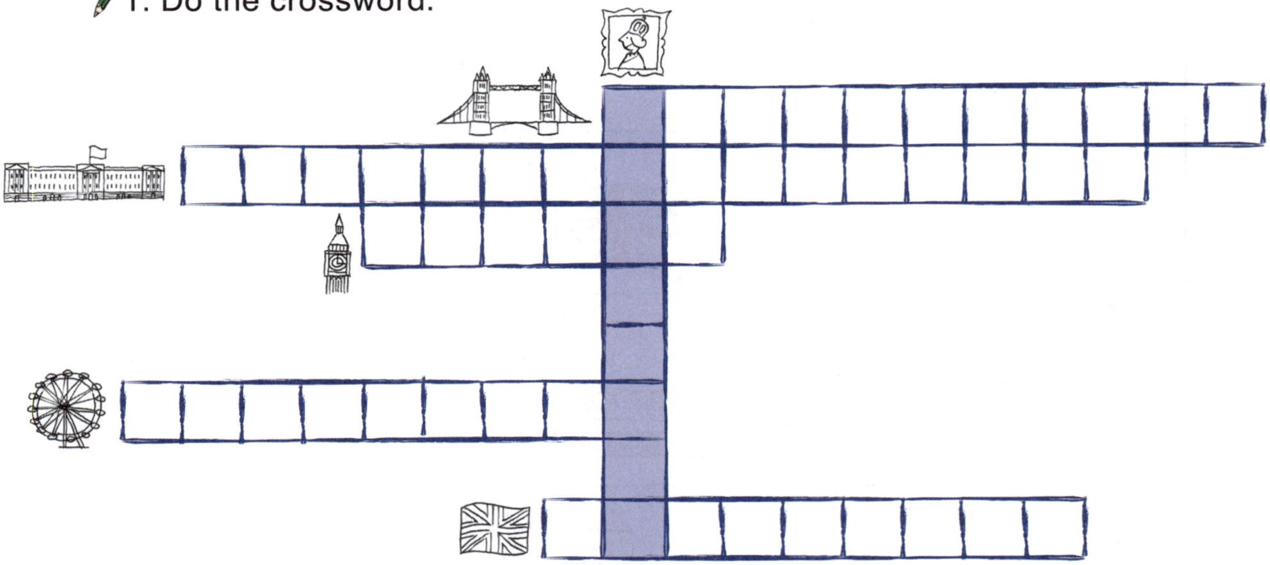

_____ lives at Buckingham Palace.

| Buckingham Palace | London Eye | Big Ben |
| Union Jack | the Queen | Tower Bridge |

2. Cross out.

The Union Jack | The London Eye | is a big 🎡.

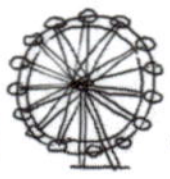

The London Eye | Big Ben | is a 🔔.

Buckingham Palace | Tower Bridge | is the home of the .

The Union Jack | Big Ben | is the 🇬🇧 of Great Britain.

3. Correct or wrong? Circle the letters and write down the word.

	correct	wrong
Sally and Koala are in New York.	C	F
Sally and Koala play hide-and-seek.	L	B
Sally and Koala visit the Queen.	N	A
Sally and Koala go by bus.	G	E

4. Look and write.

_____ is on the _____ .

_____ is at _____ .

_____ is at _____ .

Schau dir nochmal den Comic an. Schreibe auf, wer von beiden sich bei der abgebildeten Sehenswürdigkeit versteckt hat. Schreibe auch den Namen der Sehenswürdigkeit auf.

Look at the comics again. Find the correct answer and write down the letter. What can you read?

A frogs	**H** cold and rainy	**T** too short	**T** sunshine	**A** five
L scared	**E** pink	**N** Bucking-ham Palace	**R** rainbow	**M** book
I racing car	**T** horse	**I** Koala	**N** ten	**S** hot chocolate
S too long	**G** grey	**G** straw-berry jam	**E** dog	**!** London Eye

Comic Seite 3:   What colour are Sally's ears?
Comic Seite 6:   How many lollipops does Billy buy?
Comic Seite 9:   What colour does Sally use for her picture?
Comic Seite 12:   How does Lilly feel?
Comic Seite 15:   What toy does the boy want?
Comic Seite 18:   Sally's red skirt is ….
Comic Seite 21:   What's the weather like on Thursday?
Comic Seite 24:   Who's Sally's best friend?
Comic Seite 27:   What's Betty's favourite drink?
Comic Seite 30:   What does Sally put into her glass of milk?
Comic Seite 33:   What does Lucy eat?
Comic Seite 36:   What pet has the girl got?
Comic Seite 39:   Sally loves catching …
Comic Seite 42:   The boy thinks it's easy to ride a …
Comic Seite 45:   You can have a look over London from it.

Now colour the fields with the correct answers. What can you see?   I can see a ☐ ☐ ☐ ☐ ☐